Aug 2014

Richard Sherman

By Jon M. Fishman

AMAZING ATHLETES

Lerner Publications

Lerner Publications Company
A division of Lerner Publishing Group, Inc.
241 First Avenue North
Minneapolis, MN 55401 USA

For reading levels and more information, look up this title at www.lernerbooks.com.

Library of Congress Cataloging-in-Publication Data

Fishman, Jon M.
     Richard Sherman / by Jon M. Fishman.
          pages cm. — (Amazing athletes)
     Includes index.
     ISBN 978–1–4677–5699–0 (lib. bdg. : alk. paper)
     ISBN 978–1–4677–5701–0 (eBook)
     1. Sherman, Richard, 1988– 2. Football players—United States—Biography. I. Title.
GV939.S44F57 2015
     796.332092—dc23 [B]   2014009374

Manufactured in the United States of America
1 – BP – 7/15/14

TABLE OF CONTENTS

Richard Sherman gets focused during the Seattle Seahawks' 2014 NFC Championship game.

SUPER BOWL BOUND

Richard Sherman of the Seattle Seahawks ran backward. His long hair flapped around his helmet. Then he spun and began running forward to keep up with San Francisco 49ers **wide receiver** Michael Crabtree. The ball wasn't thrown in their direction. Richard wasn't surprised.

The two teams were playing in Seattle on January 19, 2014. The winner would be **conference** champion and go to the Super Bowl. Voices in the crowd shook the stadium at every big play. Seahawks fans are some of the loudest in the world.

Excited fans fill CenturyLink Field in Seattle, Washington, to cheer on the Seahawks.

Colin Kaepernick of the 49ers *(right)* runs the ball while Richard attempts a tackle.

Richard is one of the best **cornerbacks** in the National Football League (NFL). He stays close to his opponents' wide receivers, so quarterbacks often look for easier targets. Richard loves to remind them of that on the field. "I'll go say something to the quarterback," Richard said. "I'm like, 'Hey man, I'm over here. Don't be scared to throw it my way from time to time.'"

The 49ers had the lead after three quarters, 17–13. But Seattle scored 10 points in the fourth quarter to jump ahead 23–17. The 49ers took control of the ball with only a few minutes left on the game clock. If they could score a touchdown, they would win.

Jim Harbaugh is San Francisco's head coach. He coached at Stanford University when Richard went to school there.

Richard (left) stays close to 49ers wide receiver Michael Crabtree (right).

San Francisco **quarterback** Colin Kaepernick drove his team down the field. With less than a minute left in the game, he threw a long pass to Crabtree in the **end zone**. San Francisco was challenging Richard with the game on the line!

Richard (*right*) knocks the ball away from Michael Crabtree (*left*).

The ball soared toward the corner of the end zone. Richard and Crabtree sprinted to get there. Each player hoped to reach the end zone first. Richard snapped his head around at the last second. He raised his arm and hit the ball. It bounced to a teammate. **Interception!** The Seahawks won the game.

Richard was fired up. He was interviewed seconds after the game ended. "I'm the best cornerback in the game!" he shouted. "When you try me with a sorry receiver like Crabtree, that's the result you are going to get!" Richard has never been afraid to speak his mind.

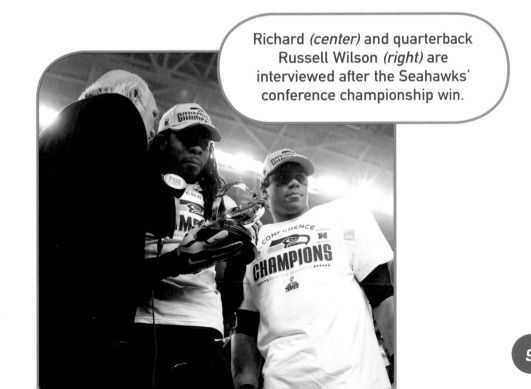

Richard (center) and quarterback Russell Wilson (right) are interviewed after the Seahawks' conference championship win.

Richard *(left)* poses with his brother, Branton *(right)*.

FOCUSED ON THE FUTURE

Richard Kevin Sherman was born in Compton, California, on March 30, 1988. He has an older brother named Branton and a younger sister named Krystina. Their parents are Beverly and Kevin.

Compton was a troubled city in the 1980s and the 1990s. It had become known for gang violence. Gang members sold drugs and fought for control of neighborhoods.

Kevin knew firsthand about Compton's problems with drugs and violence. When he was 18, he hung out with gang members. One day, a fight broke out. Kevin was shot twice. The bullets entered his chest just above his heart.

Compton is a city located in Los Angeles County, California.

Kevin was lucky to survive. The attack taught him a valuable lesson. "I realized that I had to get my act together," he said. He soon got married. Beverly helped keep him out of trouble.

The Shermans set good examples for their kids. Beverly works with children in need.

Kevin is a **sanitation worker**. He gets up for his job at 4:00 every morning. He had played football in high school.

Like this young boy, Richard started playing football at an early age.

He passed his love for the sport on to his sons. Kevin practiced with the boys whenever he could.

Richard took his parents' message to heart. He wanted to avoid the problems that could be found outside his front door. He focused on his schoolwork and on becoming a better athlete. Richard's efforts paid off. He stayed out of trouble and got good grades. He also started to become a very good football player.

In 2002, Richard started school at Dominguez High School as a first-year student. Teachers and coaches could tell right away that he was different. "He read a lot," said his high school football coach, Keith Donerson. "His vocabulary was totally different . . . and the other kids teased him about it."

STUDENT ATHLETE

Richard didn't mind being teased. He was set on bettering himself. Jeron Johnson played with Richard on the Dominguez football team. The two later played together in Seattle. "He was one of the smartest dudes at our school," Johnson said of Richard. "He knew what he wanted to do. While we were fooling around, he was focused on his books."

He was interested in sports too. In middle school, Richard had played baseball and basketball in addition to football. When he got to Dominguez, he also joined the track-and-field team. His brother, Branton, was a senior at the school in 2002. He ran track, so Richard followed in Branton's footsteps.

Richard competes during a high school track meet.

Trying other sports was fun, but Richard had the skills and drive to become a special football player. He played cornerback at Dominguez, just as he would in the NFL years later. He also returned **kickoffs** and **punts**. But his best position was wide receiver.

Richard kept working in the classroom and on the field. He was one of the top students in his class. He

Richard played cornerback on his high school team.

also caught 13 touchdown passes as a senior in 2005 and ran for one more. He was strong at cornerback too and continued to return kicks. In track and field, he won the state championship in the **triple jump** event.

Cornerbacks and wide receivers rely on their speed. If they can't run fast enough, other players will beat them to the ball. Richard is a fast runner. But he usually isn't the fastest runner on the field. Still, he was sure he had the size and skills to play at the next level. He was more than 6 feet tall by 2005. And he had shown at Dominguez that he knew what to do to succeed on a football field.

As a high school student, Richard competed in the 2005 CaliFlorida Bowl.

"COMPTON TO STANFORD"

The CaliFlorida Bowl was a game held each year for some of Florida and California's best high school football players. In 2005, Anaheim, California, hosted the game. Well-known high school players, such as Florida's Tim Tebow, were taking part. Richard agreed to play for the California team. He thought it could help him attract interest from colleges.

Richard impressed the California coaches and other players during practices. He showed the skills needed to play in college. And he was certainly tall enough at 6 feet 2 inches. Florida won the game 24–22.

Tim Tebow played against Richard at the CaliFlorida Bowl. Tebow later became an NFL quarterback.

The future NFL star was drawing a lot of attention from college football teams after the CaliFlorida Bowl. But as always, Richard balanced sports and school. Pete Carroll was the head football coach at the University of Southern California (USC) at the time. He went to Dominguez to visit Richard. The coach had to wait for more than two hours because Richard wouldn't leave class early. Richard graduated in the spring of 2006 as the class

Coach Pete Carroll was determined to have Richard play for Stanford University.

salutatorian—the student with the second-best grades.

Making Coach Carroll wait didn't hurt Richard's chances with USC. The school offered him a **scholarship** to play football. So did other colleges. Richard chose Stanford University in Stanford, California.

Stanford is known for its high learning standards. It also has a good football team. But Richard's brother, Branton, thought he should go to USC. It had the best college football team in the country at the time. Richard was sure of his choice, though. "I had to prove it was possible: Compton to Stanford," he said.

Pete Carroll left USC and became the head coach of the Seattle Seahawks. He was Seattle's coach when the team won the Super Bowl in 2014.

Richard immediately became Stanford's best wide receiver. He led the team with 34 catches in 2006. He did even better in 2007 with 39 catches. But in 2008, Richard went down early in the season with a serious knee injury.

Richard pushes for the ball in a game against San Jose State University.

After a knee injury, Richard took time to heal and rest before returning to football in 2009.

RICHARD THE GREAT

Richard missed most of the 2008 season. He sat on the bench as a **red shirt** and healed. When he returned to the field in 2009, Richard switched to cornerback. The change was for the better. Richard's height made it hard for quarterbacks to get the ball past him. He had also grown strong. Players on other teams knew him as a tough **defender**.

The young star had two good seasons at Stanford as a cornerback. In 2010, he earned his **degree**. It was time to move on to the NFL.

The concerns about Richard's running speed had not gone away. He sat through the first  round of the 2011 NFL **Draft** without hearing his name called. No team chose him in round 2, either. Player after player was chosen, and still Richard didn't get the call. Finally,

Richard runs the 40-yard dash in front of NFL coaches before the 2011 NFL Draft.

in the fifth round, Seattle opted for the big cornerback from Stanford. In all, 153 players were taken before Richard.

He didn't understand why so many teams had passed on him. "By the time the fifth round rolled around, the damage was done," he said. He vowed to make teams pay for their mistakes.

Richard makes a catch before the 2011 NFL Draft.

Since joining the NFL, Richard has become one of the best defenders in the league. And after beating the 49ers in 2014, Richard and Seattle went on to crush the Denver Broncos in the Super Bowl 43–8.

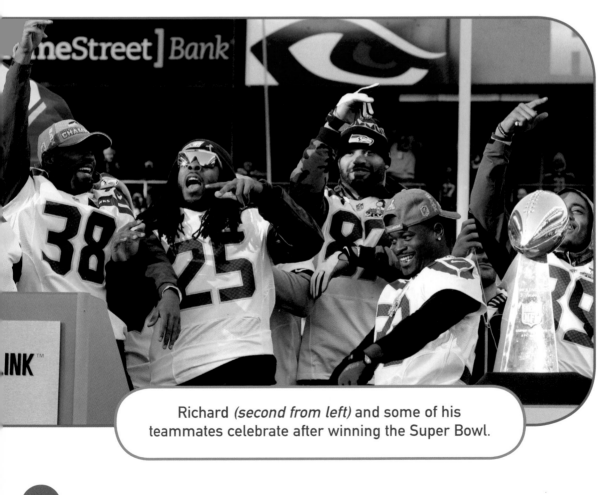

Richard *(second from left)* and some of his teammates celebrate after winning the Super Bowl.

NFL wide receivers know Richard for his physical style and a mouth that never seems to stop moving. Sometimes his mouth can get him in trouble. Many people were upset with the way he talked about Crabtree after the **playoff** game in 2014. He later apologized.

Richard talks to reporters with a smile on his face during Super Bowl media day in 2014.

Richard shakes hands with a fan on Super Bowl media day.

Richard is much more than just the fiery player fans see on TV. He is smart and thoughtful. He spends time and money helping students at Dominguez High School reach their dreams. "If you're not helping people, what are you doing?" he has said. Next season, he'll try to help the Seahawks win the Super Bowl again.

Selected Career Highlights

2013–2014 Helped the Seattle Seahawks win the Super Bowl
Ranked first in the NFL with eight interceptions
Voted to NFL Pro Bowl

2012–2013 Ranked second in the NFL with eight interceptions

2011–2012 Chosen in fifth round of NFL draft
Recorded 46 tackles and four interceptions for Seattle

2010–2011 Recorded 50 tackles and four interceptions for Stanford

2009–2010 Switched positions and became a cornerback
Recorded 62 tackles and two interceptions for Stanford

2008–2009 Missed most of season with knee injury

2007–2008 Caught 39 passes and scored four touchdowns for Stanford

2006–2007 Caught 34 passes and scored three touchdowns for Stanford

2005–2006 Caught 13 touchdown passes and ran for one touchdown for
Dominguez
Played in CaliFlorida Bowl
Won state championship in triple jump
Became salutatorian of his high school class

2004–2005 Caught four touchdown passes and ran for one touchdown
for Dominguez

2003–2004 Played three positions on Dominguez
football team: wide receiver,
cornerback, and kick returner

2002–2003 Played four sports at Dominguez High
School: baseball, basketball, football,
and track and field

Glossary

conference: a group of college sports teams that play against one another

cornerbacks: football players whose main job is to stop the other team from completing passes

defender: a player who tries to keep the other team from scoring

degree: a title given to a student after he or she completes an area of study

draft: a yearly event in which teams take turns choosing new players from a group

end zone: the area beyond the goal line at each end of a football field. A team scores a touchdown when they reach the other team's end zone.

interception: a forward pass that is caught by the other team. The team that caught the interception takes control of the ball.

kickoffs: kicks that put the ball into play. A kickoff results in the opposing team getting control of the ball.

playoff: one game in a series of games held to determine a champion

punts: kicks to the football after it is dropped and before it hits the ground. A punt results in the opposing team getting control of the ball.

quarterback: a football player whose main job is to throw passes

red shirt: a college athlete who is kept out of competition for a year. Red shirts can extend their time playing sports in college by one year.

salutatorian: the student who finishes with the second-best grades in his or her class

sanitation worker: a person who collects garbage and takes it away

scholarship: money awarded to a student to help pay for college

triple jump: a track-and-field event in which athletes jump as far as possible

wide receiver: a football player whose main job is to catch passes

Further Reading & Websites

Fishman, Jon M. *Colin Kaepernick*. Minneapolis: Lerner Publications, 2015.

Kennedy, Mike, and Mark Stewart. *Touchdown: The Power and Precision of Football's Perfect Play*. Minneapolis: Millbrook Press, 2010.

NFL Website
http://www.nfl.com
The NFL's official website provides fans with recent news stories, statistics, biographies of players and coaches, and information about games.

Savage, Jeff. *Tim Tebow*. Minneapolis: Lerner Publications, 2013.

Seattle Seahawks Website
http://www.seahawks.com
The official website of the Seahawks includes team schedules, news, profiles of past and present players and coaches, and much more.

Sports Illustrated Kids
http://www.sikids.com
The *Sports Illustrated Kids* website covers all sports, including football.

LERNER

SOURCE

Expand learning beyond the printed book. Download free, complementary educational resources for this book from our website, www.lerneresource.com.

Index

Photo Acknowledgments

The images in this book are used with the permission of: AP Photo/Paul Jasienski, p. 4; AP Photo/Gregg Trott, p. 5; © Otto Greule Jr/Getty Images, p. 6; © Ronald Martinez/Getty Images, pp. 7, 9; AP Photo/The Sacramento Bee, Hector Amezcua, p. 8; © Michael Buckner/Getty Images, p. 10; © Kevork Djansezian/Getty Images, p. 11; © iStockphoto.com/dswebb, p. 12; AP Photo/ Bob Leverone, p. 14; Marin Media/Cal Sport Media/Newscom, p. 15; © Heston Quan/Maxpreps.com, p. 16; © Joshua Thompson/Maxpreps.com, p. 18; AP Photo/G. Newman Lowrance, p. 19; AP Photo/Paul Conners, p. 20; Daniel R. Harris/Icon SMI/Newscom, pp. 22, 29 Image of Sport Photos/ Newscom, p. 23; AP Photo/Darron Cummings, pp. 24, 25; AP Photo/Ted S. Warren, p. 26; JASON SZENES/EFE/Newscom, p. 27; John Angelillo/UPI/ Newscom, p. 28.

Front cover: Rich Kane/Newscom

Main body text set in Caecilia LT Std 55 Roman 16/28.
Typeface provided by Adobe Systems.